Words Their Way

Word Sorts for Letter Name–Alphabetic Spellers

Francine Johnston
University of North Carolina, Greensboro

Marcia Invernizzi
University of Virginia

Donald R. Bear
University of Nevada, Reno

PEARSON

Merrill
Prentice Hall

Upper Saddle River, New Jersey
Columbus, Ohio

Library of Congress Cataloging-in-Publication Data

Words their way : word sorts for letter name–alphabetic spellers / Francine Johnston . . . [et al.].—1st ed.
   p. cm
  ISBN 0-13-183813-X
   1. Word recognition. 2. English language—Orthography and spelling. I. Johnston, Francine R.

LB1050.44.W68 2004
372.63'2—dc21

2003044929

Vice President and Executive Publisher: Jeffery W. Johnston
Senior Editor: Linda Ashe Montgomery
Editorial Assistant: Laura Weaver
Development Editor: Hope Madden
Production Editor: Mary M. Irvin
Production Coordination: Amy Gehl, Carlisle Publishers Services
Design Coordinator: Diane C. Lorenzo
Illustrations: Francine R. Johnston
Cover Designer: Ali Mohrman
Cover Image: Jean Claude Lejuene
Production Manager: Pamela D. Bennett
Director of Marketing: Ann Castel Davis
Marketing Manager: Darcy Betts Prybella
Marketing Coordinator: Tyra Poole

This book was set in Palatino by Carlisle Communications, Ltd. It was printed and bound by Phoenix Color Corporation. The cover was printed by Phoenix Color Corporation.

Pearson Education Ltd.
Pearson Education Singapore Pte. Ltd.
Pearson Education Canada, Ltd.
Pearson Education—Japan

Pearson Education Australia Pty. Limited
Pearson Education North Asia Ltd.
Pearson Educación de Mexico, S.A. de C. V.
Pearson Education Malaysia Pte. Ltd.

10 9 8 7 6 5 4 3
ISBN: 0-13-183813-X

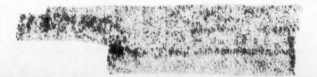

Preface

Words Their Way: Word Sorts for Letter Name–Alphabetic Spellers is intended to supplement the text *Words Their Way: Word Study for Phonics, Vocabulary, and Spelling Instruction*. That core text provides a practical, research-based and classroom-proven way to study words with students. This supplemental text expands and enriches that word study, specifically for letter name–alphabetic spellers.

Letter name–alphabetic spellers are typically beginning readers. They have progressed beyond making random marks and representational drawings in their writing, and are generally using initial and final consonants with some consistency in both reading and writing. They are ready to begin the study of blends and digraphs through picture sorts, word families, and short vowels in CVC patterns.

Words Their Way: Word Sorts for Letter Name–Alphabetic Spellers provides teachers with prepared reproducible sorts and step-by-step directions on how to guide students through the sorting lesson. There are organizational tips as well as follow-up activities to extend the lesson through weekly routines. The materials provided in this text will complement the use of any existing phonics, spelling, and reading curricula.

More resources for word study in the letter name–alphabetic stage, including additional spelling inventories for grades 1-3, resources for using word study with students who speak Spanish, links to website relating to word study, as well as news about the *Words Their Way* CD-ROM and Video, and other supplementary materials and word study events, can be found on the text's Companion Website. You can link to this site at

www.prenhall.com/bear

Contents

Overview

This collection of sorts includes both pictures and words for students who are in the letter name–alphabetic stage of spelling. Chapter 5 in *Words Their Way: Word Study for Phonics, Vocabulary, and Spelling* (Bear, Invernizzi, Templeton, & Johnston, 2003) describes this stage in detail. Chapter 2 describes how to assess your students to determine their instructional level. Most letter name–alphabetic spellers are usually in late kindergarten and first grade and should know how to hear and spell most consonant sounds in preparation for the features in this book. A quick review of initial consonants is provided first in five lessons. Same-vowel word families are then introduced with words and pictures and then digraphs and blends are covered using picture sorts. Word families are revisited in mixed-vowel contrasts and include words with digraphs and blends. Students then focus on the short vowel itself in sorts that move beyond families and continue to review digraphs and blends in CVC words. Finally there is a brief introduction to *r*-influenced vowels compared to short vowels and a simple contraction sort.

For each set of sorts there are *Notes for the Teacher* and suggestions to introduce and practice the sorts. Sorts are presented as blackline masters that can be reproduced for every child. It is important that each child sort his or her own words several times. You may want to enlarge the pages in this book slightly to increase the size of the pictures or words and reduce the amount of trimming students need to do when cutting out the sorts. You can also use the masters to prepare a set of pictures and words for modeling. You may want to make a transparency of the sort and cut it apart for use on an overhead or enlarge the pictures for use in a pocket chart. You can also simply make your own copy to cut apart and use on a desktop or on the floor. See *Words Their Way (WTW)* and the *Words Their Way CD-ROM* (WTWCD) for additional background information, organizational tips, games, and activities.

The pacing for these sorts is designed for slow to average growth. After introducing a sort you should spend three to five days following routines that encourage students to practice for mastery. However, if your students seem to be catching on quickly you can speed up the pace by spending fewer days on a sort or you may skip some sorts altogether. However, you may need to slow down and perhaps even create additional sorts for some students using pictures from *WTW* and word lists throughout this book and in *WTW*. Templates to create these additional sorts can be found in *WTW* and at the end of this book.

SORTS 1-5

Review Sorts for Initial Consonants

NOTES FOR THE TEACHER

These five picture sorts are designed to quickly review the initial consonants. Such a review may be especially useful for first graders at the beginning of the year. Students who are still confusing many initial consonants probably need a slower pace, but if students have missed only one or two consonants on a spelling inventory and you see that they are representing most consonants correctly in their writing, then a fast-paced review may be all that is needed. You may also want to use the Spell Check on page 11 for a pretest to see which children really need such a review. Additional review will take place as students work with word families.

STANDARD WEEKLY ROUTINES FOR USE WITH SORTS 1-5

1. **Repeated Work with the Pictures:** Students should repeat the sort several times after it has been modeled and discussed under the teacher's direction. Make a copy of the blackline master for each student, enlarging it to reduce paper waste and increase the size. After cutting out the pictures and using them for individual practice, the pieces can be stored in an envelope or baggie to sort again several times on other days. See *WTW* for tips on managing picture sorting.
2. **Draw and Label and Cut and Paste:** For seatwork, students can draw and label pictures of things that begin with the target sounds/letters. They can also look for pictures in magazines and catalogs and paste those into categories by beginning sound. The pictures from the blackline sort can be pasted into categories and children can be asked to label the pictures. This can serve as an assessment tool but *do not* expect accurate spelling of the entire word at this time.
3. **Word Hunts and Word Banks:** Students can look through their word banks and reading materials for words that have the targeted consonant sounds and record these. Plan a time for sharing their findings.
4. **Games and Other Activities:** Many games are described in *WTW* and are available to print out from the WTWCD. Variations of the "Follow the Path" game work especially well with beginning consonants. You might want to create one for each of the five sorts presented here.

SORTS 1–5 BEGINNING CONSONANT SOUNDS
Demonstrate, Sort, Check, and Reflect

1. Prepare a set of pictures to use for teacher-directed modeling. Use the letter cards as headers and display the pictures randomly with picture side up.
2. Begin a **sound sort** by modeling one word into each column explaining explicitly what you are doing: "Here is a picture of a bug. *Bug* starts with the /b/ sound made by the letter *B* so I will put it under the picture of the BELL. This is a picture of a map. Mmmmap starts with the /m/ sound made by the letter *M* so I will put it under the picture of the MOUSE." Model a picture under R and S in the same manner and then say, *"Now who can help me sort the rest of these pictures?"* Continue with the children's help to sort all of the pictures. Let mistakes go for now. Your sort will look something like the one shown in Figure 1.
3. When all the pictures have been sorted, name them in columns and check for any that need to be changed: *"Do all of these sound alike at the beginning? Do we need to move any?"*

FIGURE 1

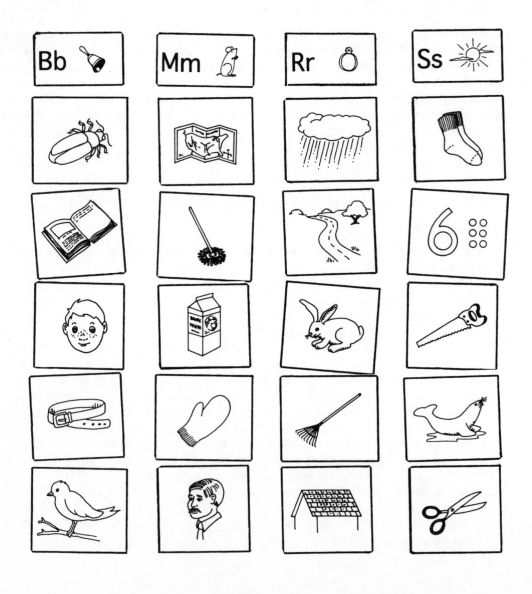

4. Repeat the sort with the group again. Keep the letter cards as headers. You may want to mix up the words and turn them face down in a deck this time and let children take turns drawing a card and sorting it in the correct column. You can also simply pass out the pictures and have the children take turns sorting them. After sorting, model how to check by naming the words in each column and then talk about how the words in each column are alike.

Extending: Give each student a copy of the sort for individual practice. Assign them the task of cutting out the pictures to match them on their own in the same way they did in the group. Give each student a plastic bag or envelope to store the pieces. On subsequent days students should repeat the sorting activity several times. Involve the students in the other weekly routines previously listed and described in *WTW* for the letter name–alphabetic stage.

ASSESSMENT OF BEGINNING CONSONANTS

All the consonants are assessed with the Spell Check for Review of Initial Consonants on page 11. This is designed for use as a pretest and/or as a posttest. To administer the assessment, name each picture and encourage children to spell as much of the word as they can even though they will only be formally assessed on the initial sound. If students are representing some of the vowels and many final consonants, then they should be ready for the study of word families. The pictures are:

1. lips	2. top	3. mat	4. kite
5. duck	6. bat	7. yell	8. game
9. rope	10. net	11. jet	12. zip
13. foot	14. pig	15. soap	16. web
17. vine	18. cup	19. ham	

SORT 1 Beginning Consonants

SORT 2 Beginning Consonants

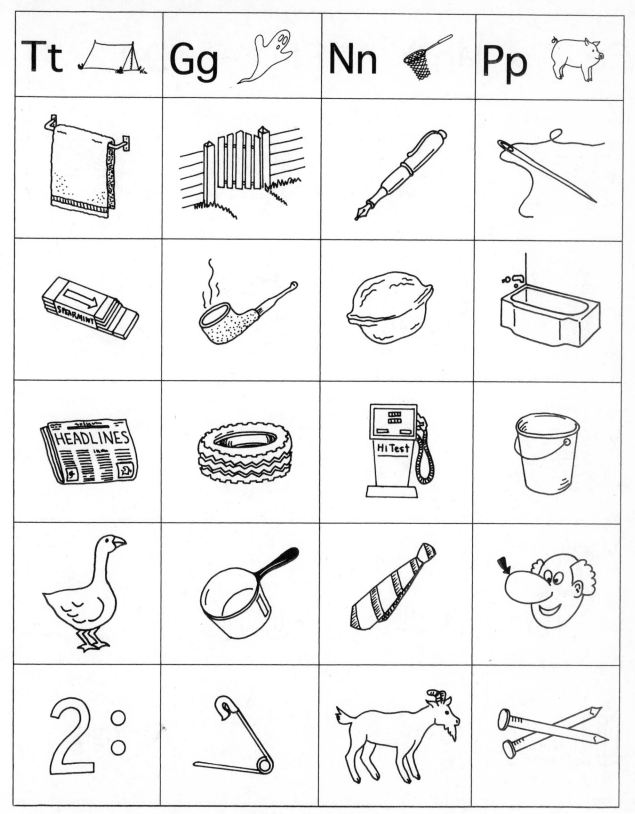

SORT 3 Beginning Consonants

SORT 5   Beginning Consonants

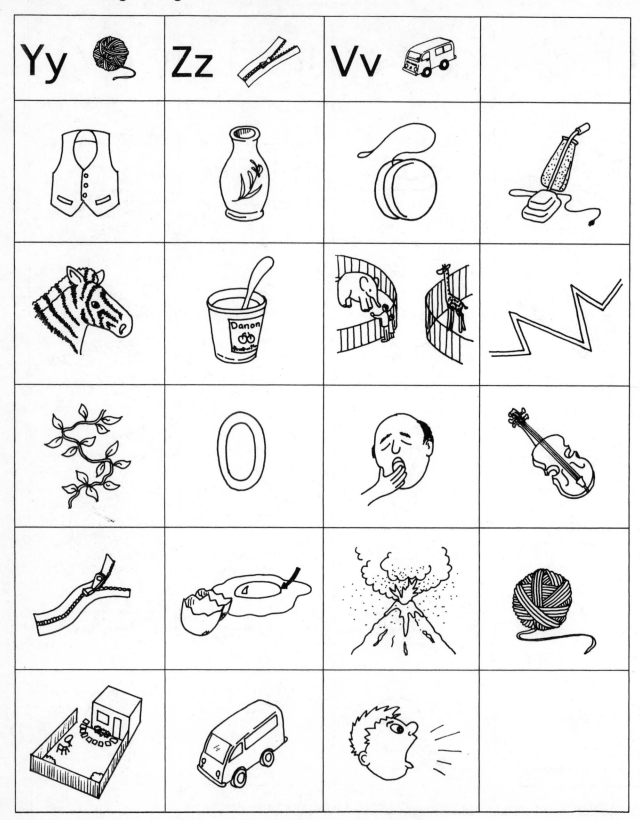

Words Their Way: Word Sorts for Letter Name-Alphabetic Spellers ©2004 by Prentice Hall, Inc.

10

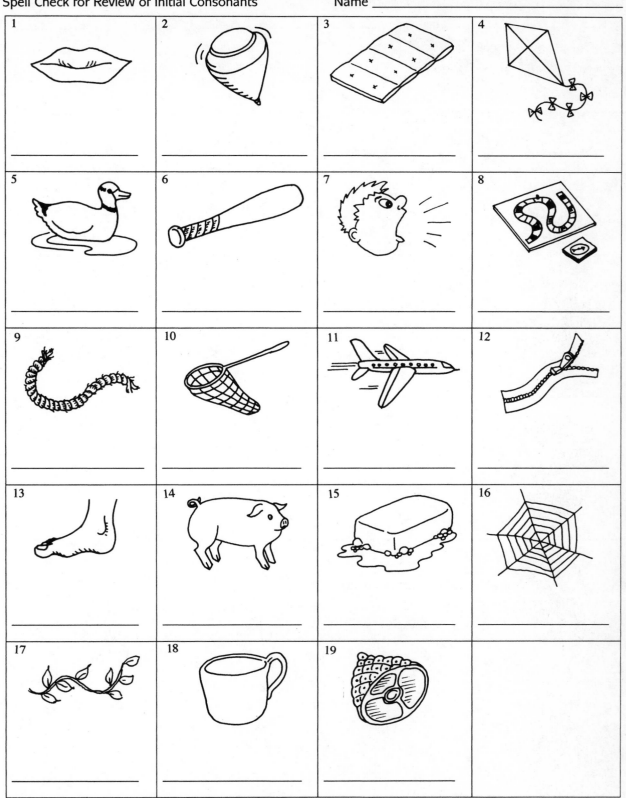

SORTS 6-12

Same-Vowel Word Families with Pictures

NOTES FOR THE TEACHER

Word families or phonograms that share the same vowel are a good way to review consonants and introduce students to short vowels and the visual aspects of rhyme. While working with word families, children will practice phonological blending skills as they learn to say the **onset,** or first sound (such as the *c* in *cat* or the *fl* in *flat*), and add on the **rime** (the vowel and what follows such as the *at* in *cat*) to figure out a word. These sorts can be used with students who have almost mastered consonants in the initial and final positions (spelling *fun* as FN or *wet* as YT) and may be including some medial vowels (as in BOT for *boat*). Typically these children are in late kindergarten and early first grade. Initial and final consonants will be reviewed in these sorts, and blends and digraphs will be introduced.

There are seven word family sorts in this section that feature words and pictures and focus on only one vowel at a time. Sorts that contrast the vowels will come later. To slow the pace, spend more time on each sort or focus on only one family at a time before comparing two families. Some different pacing scales are suggested in *WTW*.

When possible, share books that contain a number of words from the target families as a way to introduce or reinforce the families. For example, *Cat in the Hat* is a natural connection with the *at* family and *Hop on Pop* features a variety of families (both books are by Dr. Seuss). You may also have jingles and rhymes that feature two or more words in a family, such as *Jack and Jill* that uses *Jill* and *hill*. You might present these on a chart or overhead and underline target words before or after doing the sorting and activities.

STANDARD WEEKLY ROUTINES FOR USE WITH SORTS 6-12

1. **Repeated Work with the Pictures and Words:** Students should work with the featured sorts several times after the sort has been modeled and discussed as described in each following lesson. After cutting out the words and pictures and using them for individual practice, students can store the pieces in an envelope or baggie to sort again several times on other days. The pictures and words can also be used in partner activities during which children work together to read and spell the words. At some point children may glue the sort onto paper or keep it to combine with additional sorts in review lessons.

FIGURE 2

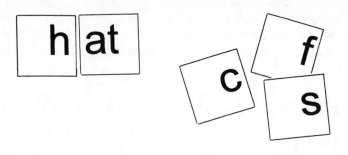

2. **Building, Blending, and Extending:** Students should be able to read and spell these words, so work on both. For building and blending, write the onsets and rimes of the target family on cards to use in a pocket chart (magnetic letters can be used as well but keep the rime unit [such as - *at*] together as a chunk).

   For **building,** say the word and then model how to make the word by putting together the onset and then the rime as shown in Figure 2. Model how to change the onset to create other words familiar from the sort. Children can work with similar materials at their places using their own letter cards (see Appendix) or a Show Me folder (described in *WTW* and available for printing from the CD-ROM).

   For **blending,** place the onset and rime in a pocket chart or write them on the board. Say the onset and then the rime as slowly as possible without distortion (e.g., /ssss/ pause /aaaat/) pointing to the *S* and then the *at* as a unit. Then say the word naturally as you run your hand under it: *sat.* Model how you can change the onset to create a new word such as *mat.* Have the students say the sounds with you and then individually. Do not isolate the vowel and the final sound. Children should learn these as a unit at this point.

   Extending: Include words in the blending activity from the list of additional words in each lesson. This will help students see that knowing a word family can help them figure out many additional words as well as the ones featured in the sort. Be aware that words with blends and digraphs will pose special challenges if students have not yet studied these features. Only a few words with blends and digraphs are included in the blackline sort at this point but more can be introduced in a group activity when the teacher can support students' efforts. This is an important way to foreshadow the work on digraphs and blends that will come next.

3. **Reading:** Use decodable texts or little books that have a number of words with the featured family. Many publishers are now creating "phonics readers," and some of them focus on word families. Be sure students can read these books with 90% accuracy on a second reading.

4. **Word Recognition:** After students have worked with the words and pictures for several days, hold up just the words and practice word recognition. Students can work in pairs to practice saying the words. Model blending of the onset and rime if students have trouble.

5. **Spelling:** Hold up pictures one at a time and have the students spell the word using letter cards, chalk boards, white boards, or pencil and paper. Ask students to underline the letters (such as *at*) that are the same in every word. Students can also work with a partner, taking turns calling a word for their partner to spell and then showing the word to check it.

6. **Word Hunts:** Look for words in daily reading that mirror the featured word families. Challenge children to find others that could go in the family or brainstorm additional words. You may want to create posters or displays of all the words students can discover for each family.

7. **Games and Other Activities:** Create flip books or word family wheels like those described in *WTW* and on the WTWCD. The Show Me game is a word-building activ-

ity we highly recommend for use with all word families. Other games such as Word Maker, Roll the Dice, and Go Fish are described in Chapter 5 of *WTW*.

8. **Assessment:** To assess student's weekly mastery, ask them to spell and read the words. A final assessment of the families covered in these sorts follows the sorts on page 27: Spell Check for Same-Vowel Word Families.

SORT 6   *AT FAMILY WITH WORDS AND PICTURES*
Demonstrate, Sort, Check, and Reflect

Prepare a set of pictures and words to use for teacher-directed modeling.

1. Introduce the sort with a **matching activity.** Arrange the pictures in a column beginning with the most familiar words such as *cat* or *hat*. Have the students join in as you name them from top to bottom. Ask the students how those words are alike. If no one mentions that they rhyme you should supply that term: "These words *rhyme.*"

2. Then arrange the word cards randomly below or off to the side where everyone can see them. Name the first picture and ask, "Can someone find the word *cat?* How did you know that word was *cat?* Yes it starts with a *c.*" Follow this procedure until all the words are matched to a picture as shown in Figure 3.

FIGURE 3

3. Read down the list of words and ask how they are alike. The idea that they rhyme should be restated as well as the idea that they all end in an *a* and a *t*. Introduce the idea that these words make up a *word family* because they all end with the same group of letters.
4. Remove the pictures. Arrange them randomly or hand them out to children in the group to match back to the words. Encourage children to tell how they could do the matching and once more ask how the words are alike.

Extending: Give each student a copy of the sort for individual practice and assign the students the task of cutting out the pictures and words to match them on their own in the same way they did in the group. Have them store their pieces in an envelope or plastic bag. On subsequent days, students should repeat the matching activity several times.

See the list of standard weekly routines for follow-up activities to the basic sorting lesson.

Additional Words: *brat, flat, scat, chat, that.*

SORT 7   AN AND AD FAMILIES WITH WORDS AND PICTURES

Demonstrate, Sort, Check, and Reflect

Prepare a set of pictures and words to use for teacher-directed modeling.

1. Introduce the pictures with a **rhyming sort.** Place the picture of the *can* and the *dad* as headers for the sort (see Figure 4). Explain that the students need to listen for rhyming words and put them under the correct picture. Select another picture such as *van.* Ask, "Does *van* rhyme with *can* or *dad*? Yes, it rhymes with *can* so we will put it under the picture of the can." Continue until all the pictures have been sorted. Have the students join in as you name them from top to bottom. Ask the students how the words in each column are alike: "These words *rhyme.*" Leave the headers and remove the other pictures. Hand out the pictures or place them randomly to the side or in a deck. Call on children individually to help sort the words again by rhyme.
2. Next introduce the word cards. Arrange them randomly below or off to the side where everyone can see them. Name the first picture and ask if someone can find that word. "Can someone find the word *can*? How did you know that word was *can*? Yes it starts with a *c* and ends with an *n*." Follow this procedure until all the words are matched to a picture. Read down the list of words in one column at a time and ask how they are alike. Children should note that they rhyme and they end in the same two letters. Remind the students that they studied the *at* family and now they are studying two more families, the *an* and *ad* families.
3. Remove the words. Arrange them randomly, put them in a deck, or hand them out to children in the group to match back to the words. Encourage children to tell how they could do the matching and once more ask how the words are alike.

Extending: See the list of standard weekly routines. In addition you can include some **review** using all three families (*at, an, ad*) using pictures and words from both sorts 1 and 2. Put out all the picture and words in a pocket chart or center and challenge students to sort into three categories.

Additional Words: *ban, Dan, tan, plan, scan, that, bad, had, lad, Brad, glad, Chad.*

FIGURE 4

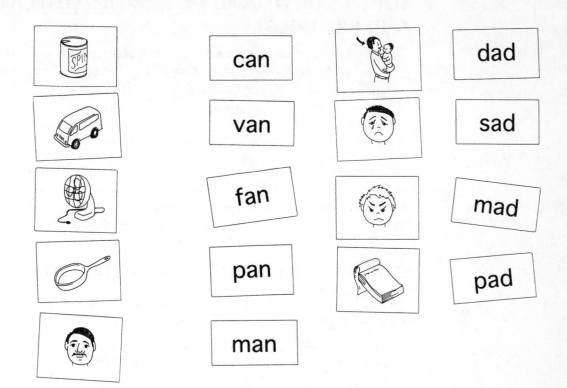

SORT 8   *AP* AND *AG* FAMILIES WITH WORDS AND PICTURES

Demonstrate, Sort, Check, and Reflect

Introduce the pictures with a rhyming sort as described for sort 7. Good headers for this sort might be *cap* and *bag*. Always be sure to ask the students how the words in each column are alike and why they are called word families.

AP words and pictures	AG words and pictures
<u>cap</u>	<u>bag</u>
lap	flag
map	rag
nap	tag
	wag

Extending: See the list of standard weekly routines. At this point you can also **review** all five *a* families (*at, an, ad, ap, ag*) using pictures and words from sorts 1, 2, and 3. Challenge students to sort into five categories. You might try this with just the words by creating your own word sort sheet. List words from all five families randomly for students to cut apart and sort by families. Follow this up with partner sorts where children take turns reading the words for their partner to sort.

Additional Words: *gap, rap, sap, tap, chap, clap, flap, scrap, slap, snap, strap, trap, wrap, gag, lag, nag, sag, brag, drag, snag, stag, shag.*

SORT 9   *OP, OT,* AND *OG* FAMILIES WITH WORDS AND PICTURES

Introduce this sort in a manner similar to that described for sort 7, except set up three headers. Sort by rhyme and then add the words. The sort will look something like this:

OP words and pictures	OT words and pictures	OG words and pictures
hop	cot	dog
top	dot	log
mop	hot	jog
pop	pot	frog

Additional Words: *bop, cop, sop, chop, crop, drop, flop, plop, prop, shop, slop, stop, got, jot, lot, not, rot, tot, blot, clot, plot, shot, slot, spot, trot, bog, cog, fog, hog, clog.*

SORT 10   *ET, EG,* AND *EN* FAMILIES WITH WORDS AND PICTURES

Introduce this sort in a manner similar to sort 7. The sort will look something like this:

ET words and pictures	EG words and pictures	EN words and pictures
net	beg	hen
jet	leg	men
pet	peg	pen
wet		ten

Additional Words: *bet, get, let, met, set, vet, fret, Meg, Greg, Ben, den, when, then.*

SORT 11   *UG, UT,* AND *UN* FAMILIES WITH WORDS AND PICTURES

Introduce this sort in a manner similar to sort 7.

UG words and pictures	UT words and pictures	UN words and pictures
bug	bun	cut
jug	run	hut
mug	sun	nut
tug		shut
rug		

Additional Words: *dug, hug, lug, pug, drug, plug, slug, chug, smug, snug, shrug, fun, gun, pun, spun, stun, but, gut, jut, rut, strut.*

SORT 12   *IP, IG*, AND *ILL* FAMILIES WITH WORDS AND PICTURES

Introduce the sort in a manner similar to sort 7.

IP words and pictures	IG words and pictures	ILL words and pictures
<u>lip</u>	<u>dig</u>	<u>hill</u>
zip	pig	mill
rip	wig	pill

Additional Words: *dip, hip, nip, sip, chip, clip, drip, flip, grip, ship, skip, slip, snip, strip, trip, whip, big, fig, gig, jig, rig, twig, bill, dill, fill, gill, ill, Jill, kill, quill, sill, till, will, chill, drill, frill, grill, skill, spill, still, thrill.*

ASSESSMENT FOR WORD FAMILIES WITH THE SAME VOWEL

The word families studied up to this point are assessed with the Spell Check for Same-Vowel Word Families on page 27. Recognition rather than production is assessed at this point, as students have not yet contrasted short vowels. Name each picture and ask students to circle the word that goes with the picture. Students can also complete this independently.

1. fan	2. hat	3. sad
4. map	5. log	6. top
7. jet	8. tag	9. cut
10. rug	11. bun	12. hill
13. dig	14. rip	15. dot

cat	mat	hat
rat	bat	fat
sat	pat	bat

fan	dad	pan
sad	man	pad
van	mad	can

nap	wag	cap
rag	map	bag
tag	flag	lap

SORT 9   *OP, OT,* and *OG* Word Families

pot	dog	cot	hop
log	frog	top	jog
mop	dot	hot	pop

Words Their Way: Word Sorts for Letter Name-Alphabetic Spellers ©2004 by Prentice Hall, Inc.

23

net	peg	jet	hen
pen	pet	beg	wet
leg	ten	men	

run	cut	mug	jug
tug	sun	hut	rug
nut	bun	shut	bug

pig	pill	wig
lip	mill	hill
dig	zip	rip

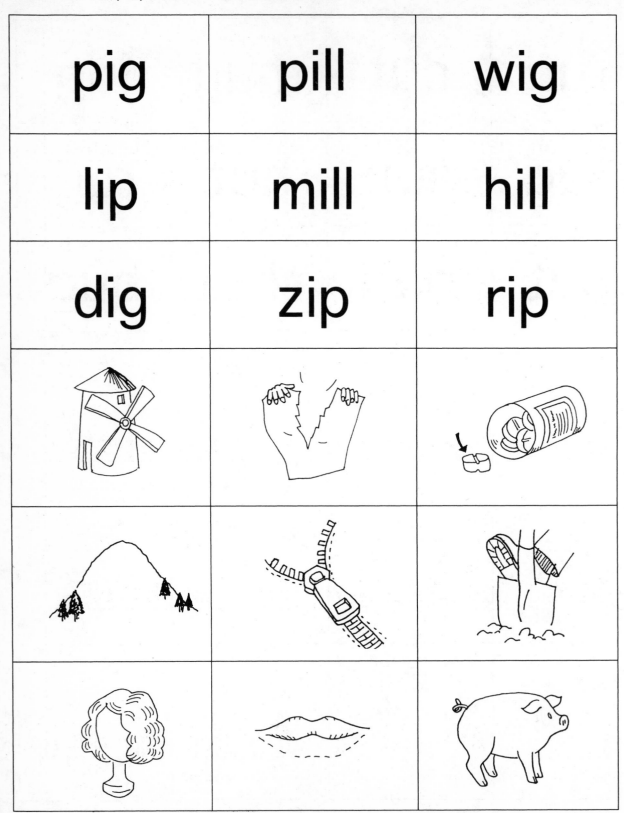

Spell Check for Same-Vowel Word Families
Circle the correct word

1 fat fan pan	**2** had hot hat	**3** sad sat mad
4 map mat mad	**5** lad log dog	**6** tap pot top
7 jet wet jog	**8** top tag rag	**9** not cat cut
10 rat rug bug	**11** bat run bun	**12** hill hit pill
13 dog dig dad	**14** rat rip rug	**15** top dog dot

Words Their Way: Word Sorts for Letter Name-Alphabetic Spellers ©2004 by Prentice Hall, Inc.

SORTS 13-26

Digraphs and Blends Picture Sorts

NOTES FOR THE TEACHER

Digraphs and blends consist of usually two and sometimes three consonants and are sometimes referred to as consonant clusters. The consonants in **blends** retain their identity but are tightly meshed with each other as in the *st* of *step*. **Digraphs,** however, are two letters that represent only one unique sound—there is no blend involved. We generally recommend teaching the term *blend* but not the term *digraph,* because blend describes what is happening in a concrete way, but digraph does not.

These sorts can be used with students who have mastered single consonants in the initial and final positions. Typically these children are in late kindergarten and early first grade. Because these sorts involve only pictures, they can be used before students have an extensive sight vocabulary of words containing blends and digraphs. The Spell Check on page 50 can be used as a pretest to determine your students' needs in this area.

Digraphs are presented first in five sorts. The first three sorts contrast *ch* and *sh* with *h* because that is often the confusion children show in their writing (i.e., *chip* may be spelled HP). All the digraphs are reviewed in sort 17 and you may skip sorts 13–16 if you think your students only need a review. Blends are covered in nine sorts. If your students seem to be catching on quickly, and this is likely to happen after you have worked with blends for several weeks, speed up your pace. Again, a slower pace is suggested in *WTW* with more intermediate steps that contrast single consonants with blends.

When possible, share books that contain a number of words with the targeted feature. For example, *Sheep in a Shop* (by Margot Apple) is a natural connection with the /sh/ sound.

STANDARD WEEKLY ROUTINES FOR USE WITH SORTS 13-26

1. **Repeated Work with the Pictures:** Students should work with the featured sorts several times after the sort has been modeled and discussed with the teacher. After cutting out the pictures and using them for individual practice, students can store the pieces in an envelope or baggie to sort again several times on other days.

2. **Word Building, Blending, and Extending:** If students have worked with the word families in sorts 1–7 they will be familiar with building and blending activities. While these sorts feature pictures and not words, each lesson will suggest possible words students can build or blend *while reviewing the families introduced previously.* For example, in the first lesson on *sh*, the words *shop, shot, shag, ship,* and *shut* can be used. Prepare a set of large cards on which you write the onset *sh* and then

the rimes needed to make each word (*op, ot, ag, ip, ut*). You can also do this with magnetic letters but keep the digraph or blend unit and rime unit together so that there are only two parts to blend into a word. For **building,** say the word and then model how to make the word by putting together the onset and then the rime. Children can then come up to make words or work with similar materials at their places (see the appendix for letter cards). For **blending,** point to the onset and then the rime saying the sounds as slowly as possible without distortion (e.g., /shshshsh/ pause /oooop/), pointing to the *sh* and then the *op* as units. Then say the word naturally as you run your hand under it: *shop*. Model how you can change the rime to create a new word: *sh-ot, sh-ip, sh-ut*. Have the students say the sounds with you and then individually.

Extending: These exercises will review word families (studied earlier) and demonstrate how those families plus knowledge of digraphs and blends can help students figure out many additional words. Keep the building and blending fast paced and use your own judgment about what words to use. *Shag* may be listed as a possible word, but it may make no sense to your students unless you can put it in a meaningful context.

3. **Draw and Label and Cut and Paste:** For seatwork, students can draw and label pictures of things that begin with the target sounds/letters. They can also look for pictures of things and paste those into categories. The pictures from the cut-up sort can be pasted into columns and children should label the pictures. Do not expect accurate spelling of the vowels at this time.

4. **Word Hunts and Word Banks:** Students can look through their word banks and reading materials for words that have the targeted blends and digraphs.

5. **Reading:** Look for little books that have a number of words with the featured digraphs and blends. Be sure students can read these books with 90% accuracy on a second reading.

6. **Games and Other Activities:** The Show Me game described in Chapter 5 can be adapted for blends and digraphs and can be used for building words. Other games are described in *WTW* and are available to print out from the WTWCD.

SORT 13   *S, H,* AND *SH* DIGRAPHS

Demonstrate, Sort, Check, and Reflect

1. Prepare a set of pictures to use for teacher-directed modeling. Use the letter cards as headers and display the pictures randomly. Begin the **sound sort** by modeling one word into each column explaining what you are doing: "Here is a picture of a hat. *Hat* starts like *hand* so I will put it under the letter *h*. This is a picture of a sheep. Shshshshsheep starts like *shovel* so I will put it under these two letters, *s-h*. Here is a sock. Ssssock starts with *s*. Now who can help me sort the rest of these pictures?" Continue with the children's help to sort all of the pictures. Let mistakes go for now. When all the pictures have been sorted, name them in columns and check for any that need to be changed: *"Do all of these sound alike at the beginning? Do we need to move any?"*

2. Repeat the sort with the group again, check, and talk about how the words in each column are alike. You may want to point out that *sh* is special because it takes two letters to spell the sound. Teaching the term *digraph* is not necessary.

S and sun	*H* and hand	*SH* and shovel
saw	horse	shirt
socks	house	ship
soap	ham	sheep
seal	hose	shark
		shoe
		shop
		shed/shack

Extending: Give each student a copy of the sort and assign them the task of cutting out the pictures and words to match them on their own in the same way they did in the group. On subsequent days students should repeat the sorting activity several times.

See the list of standard weekly routines (building, blending, and extending, reading, spelling, word hunts, etc.) for follow-up activities to the basic sorting lesson.

Additional Words for Building and Blending Made Up of Word Families Studied Earlier: *hip, sip, ship, hop, shop, hot, shot, hut, shut, shag.*

SORT 14   *C, H,* AND *CH* Digraphs

Introduce the sort in a manner similar to sort 13. Sort twice with the group. Point out that *ch* is special because it takes two letters to spell the sound.

C and cat	*H* and hand	*CH* and chair
comb	heart	cherry
coat	hat	chimney
cake	horn	chin
candy	hook	chick
		chief
		check
		chop

Additional Words: *hat, cat, chat, cap, chap, hip, chip, chill, hop, cop, chop.*

SORT 15   *H, SH,* AND *CH* DIGRAPHS

This sort reviews *sh* and *ch* and may be optional. Introduce it in a manner similar to sort 13. The sort will look something like this:

H and hand	*SH* and shovel	*CH* and chair
hat	shed / shack	cheese
hose	shop	chain
ham	sheep	chop
house	shave	chief
	shoe	chimney
		cherry

Additional Words: See sorts 13 and 14 for words with *sh* and *ch*.

SORT 16   *TH* AND *WH* DIGRAPHS

Introduce the sort in a manner similar to sort 13. Sort twice with the group. Again, you may want to point out that *wh* and *th* are special because it takes two letters to spell their sound.

Note: Children will confuse words that start with *w* and words that start with *wh*, but we do not recommend this as a picture sorting contrast because it is unlikely they can tell the difference in such words merely by sound.

TH and thumb	*WH* and wheel
thermos	wheelbarrow
thimble	whip
thirteen	whistle
thermometer	whisker
thorn	whale
think	wheel

Additional Words: *that, than, then, whip, when.*

SORT 17   *SH, CH, TH,* AND *WH* DIGRAPHS

Introduce the sort in a manner similar to sort 13. Remind children that they have sorted these before and now they are combining all four.

shovel	**chair**	**wheel**	**thumb**
shelf	cheese	whisker	thorn
shot	chick	whistle	thimble
shark	chair	whip	thirteen
shave	chain	whale	thermos
shirt	chin	wheelbarrow	
ship			

Additional Words: *ship, shop, shot, shut, shag, chat, chap, chip, chill, chop, that, than, then, whip, when.*

SORT 18   *S, T,* AND *ST* BLEND

Introduce the sort in a manner similar to sort 13, but point out that the sound for *st* is called a *blend* because the two letters work together to make the sound. Model how these sounds can be segmented: /sssss/ + /t/.

S and sun	**T and tent**	**ST and star**
six	tie	stem
sink	tire	stop
scissors	top	stump
		star
		stamp
		stick
		sting
		stir
		stool

Additional Words: *top, stop, still, sun, stun.*

SORT 19   *SP, SK,* AND *SM* BLENDS

Introduce the sort in a manner similar to sort 13, but refer to the initial consonant pairs as *blends.* Talk about how these blends all begin with *s* so they need to pay special attention to the second letter. The sort will look something like this:

SP and spider	**SK and skate**	**SM and smile**
spool	ski	smell
spoon	skull	smile
spear	skirt	smoke
spill	skeleton	
sponge	skip	
	skunk	
	skateboard	

Additional Words: *spill, spot, spun, skip, skill, smog.*

SORT 20   *SC*, *SN*, AND *SW* BLENDS

Introduce the sort in a manner similar to sort 13.

SC and scooter	SN and snail	SW and swing
school	snake	swan
scout	snap	switch
scarecrow	snowman	sweater
scarf	snow	swing
scale	snail	swim

Additional Words: *snap, snip, snug, swig.*

Review all the *s* blends with games such as the S-Blend Bingo Game on the WTWCD.

SORT 21   *P, L,* AND *PL* BLENDS

Introduce the sort in a manner similar to sort 13. This sort may be skipped if you want a faster pace. *PL* is covered in sort 22.

P and pig	L and lamp	PL and plus
pail	lock	plug
pin	log	plum
pie	leaf	plant
pan	letter	pliers
		plate
		plane
		plus

Additional Words: *pan, plan, lot, plot, lug, plug, plop.*

SORT 22   *PL*, *SL*, AND *BL* BLENDS

Introduce the sort in a manner similar to sort 13.

PL and plus	SL and slide	BL and block
plug	sled	blindfold
plum	sleeve	block
pliers	slipper	blade
plate	sleep	blouse
plane	slide	blanket

Additional Words: *plan, plot, plop, plug, blot, slap, slip, slot, slog, slug.*

SORT 23   *CR, CL, FL,* AND *FR* BLENDS

Introduce the sort in a manner similar to sort 13.

CR and crab	CL and cloud	FR and frog	FL and flag
crown	clip	fry	flower
crayon	clown	fruit	float
crib	clock	frame	fly
cry	clap	freckle	flashlight
crack	climb	freezer	
crackers			

Additional Words: *crop, clan, clap, clip, clot, frill, frog, fret, flap, flag, flip, flop.*

SORT 24   *BL, BR, GR,* AND *GL* BLENDS

Introduce the sort in a manner similar to sort 13.

BL and block	BR and broom	GR and grapes	GL and glasses
blanket	bride	grass	globe
blade	bridge	groceries	glasses
blouse	bricks	grill	glass
blockbread	grapes	glue	
blindfold	brush	grasshopper	glove

Review all the *l* blends using pictures from sorts 22, 23, and 24.

Additional Words: *brat, bran, Brad, brag, grip, grill, glad, blot.*

SORT 25   *PR, TR,* AND *DR* BLENDS

Introduce the sort in a manner similar to sort 13.

PR and present	TR and tree	DR and drum
price	trap	drill
pray	tracks	dress
prize	tractor	drip
pretzel	triangle	dream
	truck	dragon
		drive

Review all the *r* blends with pictures (sorts 23, 24, and 25) and games such as the Gruff Drops Troll at the Bridge game on the WTWCD.

Additional Words: *trap, trip, trot, drag, drip, drill, drop, drug.*

SORT 26   *K, WH, QU,* AND *TW*

Introduce the sort in a manner similar to sort 8. Note that this sort reviews the digraph *wh* and contrasts it with two blends that have the /w/ sound as part of them: *qu* and *tw*. *K* also contrasts with *qu*.

K and key	WH and wheel	QU and quilt	TW and twins
king	whip	quack	twelve
kite	whistle	quarter	twins
kick	whale	queen	twenty
key	whisker	question	
kitten	whisper	quiet	
	wheelbarrow		

Additional Words: *whip, when, quit, twig, twin.*

ASSESSMENT FOR DIGRAPHS AND BLENDS

Assess students with the Spell Check for Digraphs and Blends on page 50. Name each picture and ask students to spell the entire word. Only the beginning blend or digraph is counted right or wrong, but observe how much of the rest of the word students are able to spell. The pictures are:

1. stem	2. flag	3. smile	4. drum
5. frame	6. shot	7. snail	8. plate
9. thumb	10. swim	11. clap	12. chief
13. globe	14. wheel	15. sled	16. brush
17. grill	18. queen	19. twins	20. tree

SORT 13   *S, H,* and *SH* Digraph

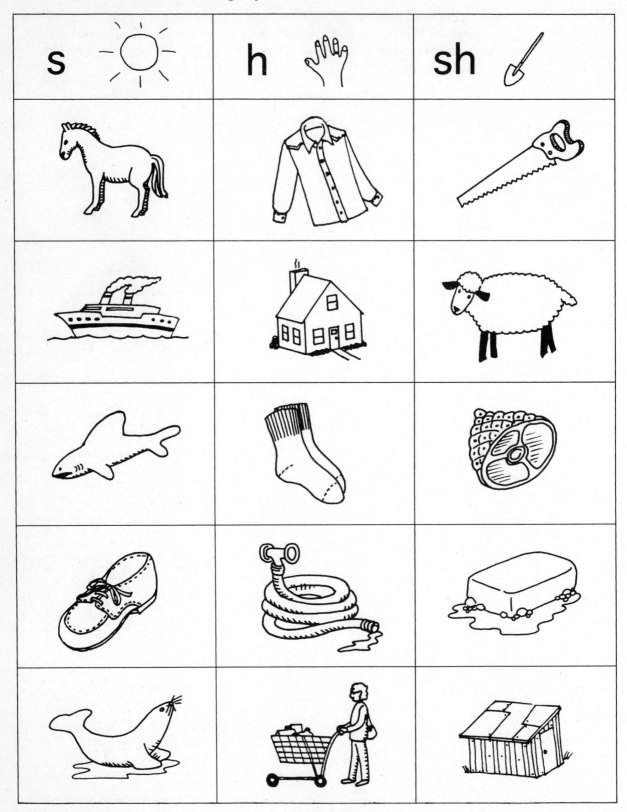

SORT 14   *C, H,* and *CH* Digraph

SORT 15   *H, SH,* and *CH* Digraphs

SORT 16   *TH*, and *WH* Digraphs

SORT 17   *SH, CH, TH, and WH Digraphs*

SORT 18   *S, T, and ST* Blend

s ☀	t ⛺	st ⭐

Words Their Way: Word Sorts for Letter Name-Alphabetic Spellers ©2004 by Prentice Hall, Inc.

41

SORT 19   *SP, SK*, and *SM* Blends

sp	sk	sm

Words Their Way: Word Sorts for Letter Name-Alphabetic Spellers ©2004 by Prentice Hall, Inc.

SORT 20 *SC, SN,* and *SW* Blends

sc	sn	sw

SORT 21   *P, L,* and *PL* Blends

p 🐷	l 💡	pl 2+1=3
(lock)	(bucket)	(apple)
(pliers)	(plug)	(pin)
(log)	(pie)	(plate)
(plane)	(plant)	(leaf)
(letter)	2+2=4	(pan)

Words Their Way: Word Sorts for Letter Name-Alphabetic Spellers ©2004 by Prentice Hall, Inc.

SORT 22 *PL*, *SL*, and *BL* Blends

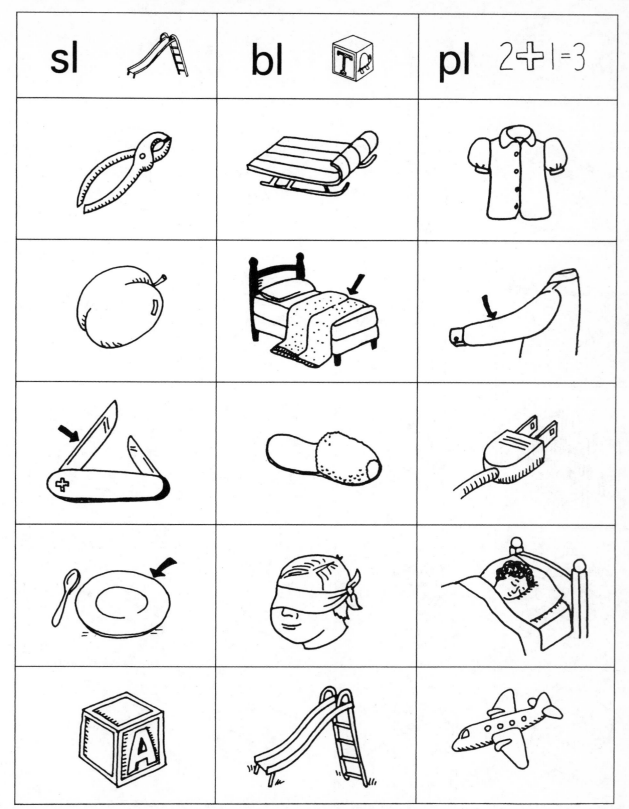

SORT 23 *CR, CL, FL,* and *FR* Blends

SORT 24   *BL, BR, GR, and GL Blends*

br (broom)	bl (block)	gr (grapes)	gl (glasses)
(bride)	(globe)	(grass shirt)	(grass)
(block A)	(bridge)	(glasses)	(groceries)
(blade)	(glass)	(grill)	(bricks)
(bread)	(bed)	(grasshopper)	(glue)
(blindfold)	(glove)	(brush)	(grapes)

SORT 25 *PR*, *TR*, and *DR* Blends

SORT 26   *K, WH, QU, and TW*

Words Their Way: Word Sorts for Letter Name-Alphabetic Spellers ©2004 by Prentice Hall, Inc.

49

Spell Check for Blends and Digraphs   Name _____

SORTS 27-33

Mixed-Vowel Word Families

NOTES FOR THE TEACHER

In these word sorts different vowels will be compared in word families or phonograms to focus students' attention on the vowel sound. Students continue to practice blending skills as they mix and match onsets (including blends and digraphs) and rimes to figure out words. This reinforces the use of analogy as a decoding strategy.

These sorts can be used with students who are using but confusing short medial vowels and representing some consonant blends and digraphs in their spelling. Typically these children are in early to middle first grade. Since theses sorts use words rather than pictures, it is important that students already know several of the words in each sort such as *cat* and *hat* in the *at* family or *hot* and *pot* in the *ot* family.

There are seven sorts that use word families to contrast vowels. Some different pacing scales and contrasts are suggested in *WTW*. There are many more word families that could be explored in similar sorts (see *WTW* for a list of word families), but by the middle of first grade most students can move on to other features once they have studied a sample of families.

When possible, share books that contain a number of words from the target families as a way to introduce or reinforce the families.

STANDARD WEEKLY ROUTINES FOR USE WITH SORTS 27-33

1. **Repeated Work with the Words:** Students should work with the featured sorts several times after the sort has been modeled and discussed in the group. Include partner work in which students read words aloud for each other to sort and spell as in no-peeking/blind sorts and writing sorts.
2. **Building, Blending, and Extending:** Students should be able to read and spell these words, so work on both building and blending as described earlier. For **blending,** use both single initial consonants and blends and digraphs (e.g., /fffllllll/ pause /aaaat/) pointing to the *fl* and then the *at* as two units to blend *flat*.
   Extending. Include words in the blending activity from the list of additional words in each lesson.
3. **Reading:** Use decodable texts or little books that have a number of words with the featured families. Be sure students can read these books with 90% accuracy on a second reading.

4. **Word Hunts:** Look for words in daily reading that mirror the featured word families. Challenge children to find others that could go in the family or brainstorm additional words. You may want to create posters or displays of all the words students can discover for each family.

5. **Games and Other Activities:** Create flip books or word family wheels like those described in *WTW* and on the WTWCD. The Show Me game is one we highly recommend for use with all word families and there are other games such as Word Maker, Roll the Dice, and Go Fish described in Chapter 5 of *WTW*.

6. **Assessment:** To assess students' mastery, ask them to spell and read the words as they are studied. A weekly spelling test might be started at this point. A final assessment follows the collection of sorts.

SORT 27   *AT, OT,* AND *IT* FAMILIES
Demonstrate, Sort, Check, and Reflect

1. Introduce the words with a **visual sort;** that is, sort first and read the words second. Use labeled pictures as headers. Explain that the students need to find more words for each word family. Model a word like *not*. Place it under *hot* and then read the header *hot* and then the word under it saying, "*Hot, not, these words go in the same family because they rhyme.*" Model several other words, and each time **sort the word first and then read** any accumulated words down from the header. Do not expect students to read the word first and then sort. They will be more successful at blending if they can use the header as a key word. As each word is sorted have the students join in as you read them from top to bottom.

2. After sorting all the words, ask the students how the words in each column are alike. Children should note that they rhyme, they are in the same family, and they end in the same two letters.

3. Discuss the meanings of the words, especially those like *bat* that mean more than one thing.

cat	hot	sit
bat	not	fit
hat	cot	bit
fat	dot	hit
mat	got	kit
pat	lot	lit
rat	pot	pit
sat	rot	
that		

4. Remove the words under each header and let the students repeat the sort together. Again, read all the words down from the top after sorting to check and encourage students to use the header and accumulating words to support their reading of unfamiliar words. Once more ask how the words are alike.

Extending: Give each student a copy of the sort to cut apart and use several times and select from the list of standard weekly routines.

Additional Words: *brat, chat, flat, scat, jot, plot, shot, spot, trot, quit, grit, skit, slit, spit.*

SORT 28   *AN, UN,* AND *IN* WORD FAMILIES

Introduce the sort in a manner similar to sort 27.

can	sun	pin
fan	run	fin
man	fun	win
tan	bun	chin
ran		thin
van		grin
pan		skin
plan		
than		

Additional Words: *an, ban, Dan, clan, scan, bin, tin, shin, spin, gun, pun, spun.*

SORT 29   *AD, ED, AB,* AND *OB* WORD FAMILIES

Introduce the words with a **visual sort** as described in sort 27 and repeat the sort together. Remember, sort first and then read all the words down from the top after sorting to encourage students to use the header and accumulating words to support their reading of unfamiliar words. Remember to discuss the meanings of such words as *tab* or *blob*.

sad	bed	crab	cob
mad	red	tab	rob
had	fed	lab	mob
bad	led	grab	sob
pad	shed	cab	job
glad	sled		blob
			glob

Additional Words: *dad, rad, lad, dab, jab, nab, blab, scab, stab, slab, wed, bled, fled, shred, gob, snob, knob.*

SORT 30   *AG, EG, IG, OG,* AND *UG* WORD FAMILIES

Introduce the sort in a manner similar to sort 27.

tag	leg	pig	dog	bug
rag	beg	dig	fog	hug
wag	peg	big	jog	rug
flag		wig	frog	plug
snag		fig	drug	
		slug		

Additional Words: *bag, sag, nag, hag, lag, brag, drag, shag, gig, jig, rig, Meg, Greg, bog, hog, log, clog, dug, lug, mug, pug, tug, chug, smug, snug, shrug.*

SORT 31   *ILL, ELL,* AND *ALL* WORD FAMILIES

Introduce the sort in a manner similar to sort 27.

pill	bell	ball
hill	tell	mall
bill	fell	fall
fill	sell	hall
mill	well	tall
will	shell	call
chill	smell	small
still		
spill		
drill		

Additional Words: *Bill, dill, Jill, kill, grill, thrill, skill, quill, cell, dell, jell, spell, swell, dwell, wall, stall.*

SORT 32   *ICK, ACK,* AND *UCK* WORD FAMILIES

Introduce the sort in a manner similar to sort 27.

chick	sack	duck
lick	tack	luck
sick	pack	tuck
tick	back	truck
pick	rack	stuck
kick	snack	
quick	black	
thick	quack	
trick	shack	
stick		

There are so many words that can be formed with these *-ck* words that it is worthwhile to spend a little extra time and create lists of all the words students can build, brainstorm, or find in their reading materials. *Ock* and *eck* words could be added in a second sort. See WTWCD for flip books.

Additional Words: *Jack, lack, Mack, crack, clack, slack, smack, stack, nick, wick, brick, click, flick, slick, buck, muck, puck, suck, cluck, pluck, shuck.*

SORT 33   *ISH, ASH,* AND *USH* WORD FAMILIES

Introduce the sort in a manner similar to sort 27.

fish	trash	brush
wish	cash	hush
dish	mash	rush
swish	rash	mush
	dash	crush
	flash	blush
	crash	flush
	smash	

Additional Words: *bash, gash, hash, lash, clash, slash, gush, lush, plush.*

ASSESSMENT FOR WORD FAMILIES WITH MIXED VOWELS

Word families are assessed with the Spell Check for Word Families that follows the collection of sorts. Name each picture and ask students to spell the word that goes with the picture. Students may not be able to complete this independently due to words such as *cash* and *sob*. Students should be able to spell the entire word correctly at this point!

1. pot	2. kit	3. fin
4. sun	5. mat	6. pan
7. rag	8. sob	9. leg
10. fall	11. hill	12. duck
13. cash	14. tack	15. dish

cat	hot	sit
not	fit	hat
bat	cot	dot
got	fat	bit
hit	mat	lot
pot	kit	pat
rat	lit	rot
pit	sat	that

can	pin	sun
run	fan	tan
man	bun	fun
fin	ran	van
pan	win	plan
chin	grin	than
skin	thin	

sad	bed	crab
cob	job	mad
red	rob	lab
had	fed	mob
sob	bad	led
pad	tab	blob
grab	shed	glad
glob	cab	sled

tag	dog	pig
bug	leg	hug
fog	dig	rag
beg	rug	big
wag	peg	wig
fig	jog	slug
flag	twig	plug
frog	drug	snag

Words Their Way: Word Sorts for Letter Name-Alphabetic Spellers ©2004 by Prentice Hall, Inc.

pill	bell	ball
fell	hill	tell
mall	bill	sell
fill	fall	hall
mill	call	will
tall	well	chill
smell	shell	still
spill	small	drill

sack	chick	duck
tack	lick	kick
luck	sick	pick
tuck	back	pack
rack	shack	tick
stuck	quick	trick
truck	thick	snack
black	quack	stick

Words Their Way: Word Sorts for Letter Name-Alphabetic Spellers ©2004 by Prentice Hall, Inc.

fish	trash	brush
cash	rush	mash
dish	hush	dash
rash	wish	mush
flash	crush	blush
swish	crash	flush
smash		

Spell Check for Mixed-Vowel Word Families   Name _____

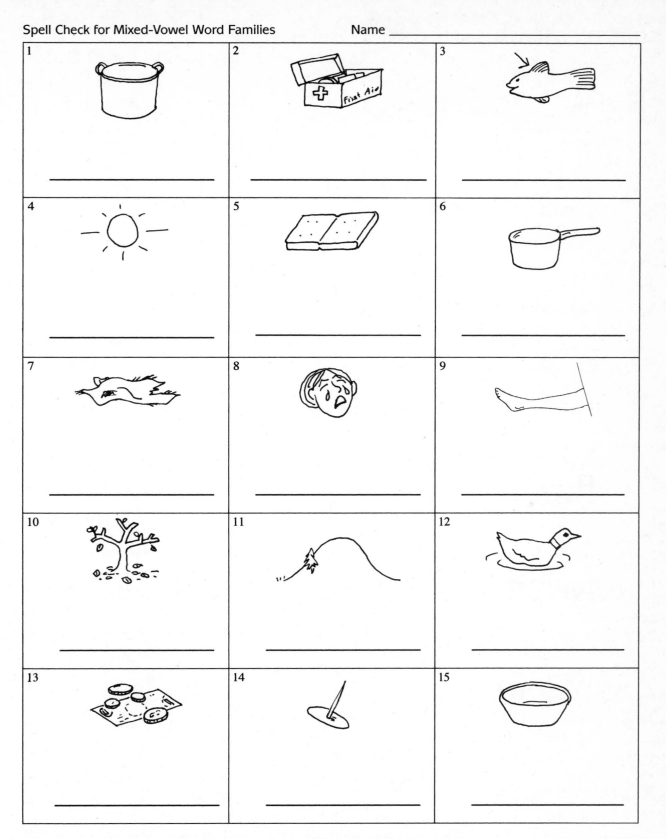

SORTS 34–37

Picture Sorts for Short Vowels

NOTES FOR THE TEACHER

In these four optional sorts, different vowels will be compared using pictures to focus students' attention to the sound of the short vowels. In earlier sorts students have had the support of word families and the printed word to make decisions about the medial vowel. With pictures, that support is removed and they must attend carefully to the sound only. These sorts can be used with students who know beginning and ending consonants but are using but confusing medial vowels. Typically these children are in early to middle first grade. You may find that these sorts are not necessary for all children.

There are four sorts that use pictures to contrast vowels. You could spend about three to five days on each sort but you can also use these during the same time you use word sorts 38 through 40 and alternate between using pictures and words. Additional sorts are on the WTWCD using different combinations of vowels.

These blackline masters might be used for assessment purposes by asking students to spell the pictured word or just the vowel in the space beside the picture.

SORT 34   SHORT *A* AND *O* PICTURES

Demonstrate, Sort, Check, and Reflect

1. Make a set of pictures to use for teacher-directed modeling in a sound sort. Use *cat* and *sock* as headers and display the pictures randomly. Begin the sort by modeling one word into each column explaining what you are doing: "Here is a picture of a flag. *Flaaaaag* has the same vowel sound in the middle as *caaaat,* so I will put it under the cat. This is a picture of a mop, *mooooop* has the same vowel sound in the middle as *soooock,* so I will put it under the sock." Continue with the children's help to sort all of the pictures. Let mistakes go for now. When all the pictures have been sorted, name them in columns and check for any that need to be changed: "Do all of these have the same vowel sound in the middle? Do we need to move any?"

2. Repeat the sort with the group, check by naming the pictures in the column, and talk about how the words are alike. The sort will look something like this:

A and cat	O and sock
flag	lock
sack	top
clap	pot
cap	fox
bag	mop
jack	box
grass	rock
can	

Extending: Give each student a copy of the sort and assign them the task of cutting out the pictures to sort as they did in the group. On subsequent days students should repeat the sorting activity.

Standard weekly routines (blending, reading, spelling) can be used as follow-up activities to the basic sorting lesson. Instead of word hunts, students might look for pictures in magazines or catalogs that have the same vowel sounds.

Students should be able to spell many of these words completely if they are familiar with the rime from the study of word families (e.g., *hill* and *wig* but not *trunk* or *grass*).

SORT 35   SHORT *I* AND *U* VOWEL PICTURES

Introduce the sort in a manner similar to sort 34. The sort will look something like this:

I and pig	*U* and cup
zip	bus
hill	sun
fin	trunk
fish	cut
lid	gum
lip	bug
wig	plus
bib	

SORT 36   SHORT *E, I, O,* AND *U* VOWEL PICTURES

Introduce the sort in a manner similar to sort 31.

E and bed	*I* and pig	*O* and sock	*U* and cup
desk	six	dot	duck
net	clip	hop	bug
vest	kick	lock	truck
leg	ship	shop	rug
sled	stick	clock	brush

SORT 37   INITIAL SHORT VOWEL PICTURES

Use the letters to set up headers. Since there are few pictures that begin with these short vowels, the ones included here are more unusual than pictures in other sorts and will need some explanation. For example, it is not likely students can identify the *otter* or the word *ick* just from the pictures. Name the pictures for the students in advance and continue to assist them in remembering what they are called. **Do not expect students to be able to spell these words.**

apple	**egg**	**igloo**
astronaut	Eskimo	itch
ax	Etch-a sketch©	in
alligator	Ed	ill
add		ick
ant		

octopus	**umbrella**
otter	up
ostrich	underwater
ox	upside down
olive	

Additional Words: Look for children's names in your class that start with these same short-vowel sounds: *Abigail, Allison, Alice, Edward, Isabell, Oscar, Oliver,* and so on. Add their names and/or pictures to the sort.

SORT 34   Short A and O Vowel Pictures

SORT 35　Short *I* and *U* Vowel Pictures

SORT 36   Short *E, I, O,* and *U* Vowel Pictures

Words Their Way: Word Sorts for Letter Name-Alphabetic Spellers ©2004 by Prentice Hall, Inc.

SORT 37   Initial Short Vowel Pictures

71

SORTS 38–47

Short Vowels in CVC Words

NOTES FOR THE TEACHER

In these word sorts, different short vowels will be compared without the support of word families. Instead students will learn to recognize the CVC pattern (consonant-vowel-consonant as in *bat* or *brat* or *blast*) in connection with the short-vowel sounds. In the next stage, within word patterns, this CVC pattern will be compared with long-vowel patterns.

Expect that students who are familiar with sorting by families may be a little confused at first when they are asked to focus just on the vowel. Modeling the sort several times will help them learn where to direct their attention.

It is important that students already know most of the words in each sort and many of the words studied earlier in word families will reappear here. There may be words students do not recognize at first and you must use your judgment about whether to keep those words in the sort (if there are only two or three this may be a good idea) or remove them and/or substitute more familiar ones. Since there are 20 or so words in a sort some can be eliminated. Harder words are generally at the bottom of the word sort sheet. After "easy" CVC words that are spelled with just single consonants, blends and digraphs will be reviewed and final preconsonantal nasals introduced (these are a type of blend that contains an *n* or *m* before another consonant: *-ng, -mp, -nt, -nd, -nk*).

Oddballs are introduced for the first time and the first two sorts have a special header card to draw attention to the new category (later ones do not have this header but you can create one if you feel it is needed). There may be one or two words in a lesson that look like they have one of the featured sounds but do not.

These sorts can be used with students in the late letter name stage who are using but confusing medial vowels, consonant blends, and digraphs. Typically these children are in middle to late first grade and should know how to read a lot of CVC words already from their reading. These sorts may also be used for review of short vowels at the beginning of second grade, or with any students who need work on short vowels, blends, or digraphs.

There are 10 sorts that contrast short vowels. If you think students only need a review of short vowels before moving on to long vowels, select the sorts that seem most appropriate and do not do all 10. If you think that your students need more practice with short vowels, there are additional words listed for each sort that can be written on the blank template at the end of the book.

Use books for instruction that feature a number of CVC words so that children will see these words in the context of reading and have the opportunity to practice them. Many publishers are creating phonics readers or decodable text that can complement the study of short vowels. A spell check can be found on page 92. This can be used as a pretest or posttest for mastery.

STANDARD WEEKLY ROUTINES FOR USE WITH SORTS 38–47

1. **Repeated Work with the Words:** Students should work with the featured sorts several times after the sort has been modeled and discussed in the group. No-peeking/blind sort and writing sorts with a partner (described in Chapter 3 of *WTW*) are especially important so that students focus on sound as well as what they see in the printed word.

2. **Word Building, Blending, and Extending:** Activities may now isolate the vowel to explore the CVC pattern in which there are three units to blend or spell as in *fl-a-sh*.

3. **Reading:** Use decodable texts or little books that have a number of words with the featured vowel sounds. Be sure students can read these books with 90% accuracy on a second reading.

4. **Word Hunts:** Look for words in daily reading materials that mirror the featured vowel sounds. Word hunts (see Chapter 3 of *WTW*) can extend children's understanding when they include longer words such as *mitten* or *tablet* that have short-vowel sounds in one or more syllables.

5. **Games and Other Activities:** The Show Me game is still a good activity for short vowels, but the focus may be more upon changing vowel sounds than upon changing the onset as was done with word families. Look for other games in Chapter 5 of *WTW* as well as the WTWCD.

6. **Homework:** If you have not established homework routines, this is a good place to start. See Chapter 3 of *WTW* for an example of a parent letter that you can send home to guide parents in reinforcing the classroom practice. See the Appendix for a worksheet that students can use independently at home.

7. **Assessment:** A weekly spelling test may become part of your routine by the late letter name stage. You may also want to select words from the additional word list for testing to see how well students can transfer their mastery of features.

SORT 38   SHORT A AND O IN EASY CVC WORDS

Demonstrate, Sort, Check, and Reflect

Prepare a set of words to use for teacher-directed modeling. Many teachers make a transparency to cut apart and model sorting on the overhead projector. This sort might be used in connection with the short vowel picture sort 34.

1. Display the words and begin by asking the students to read over them to see if there are any they do not know or understand. Help them read and discuss the meaning of any that are unfamiliar.

2. Pull out the labeled headers *cat* and *sock*. Introduce the third header "**oddball**." Explain to the students that sometimes words do not have the sound we expect or do not have the same sound as the other words in the sort. In this sort there will be two oddballs.

3. Model a word such as *sad*. Place it under *cat*, reading the header and the word under it saying, *"Saaaad, caaaat—these words have the same vowel sound in the middle."* (You can isolate the vowel by covering the letters in the word as you say *cat, at, a.*) Model several other words by reading the word and comparing it to the two headers. Include one of the two oddballs (*was, for*) in your modeling, demonstrating how the word does not have either sound in the headers. Place it in the oddball category, leaving the other oddball for the students to discover.

4. Begin calling on students to decide where to place the other words. After sorting all the words, read them from the top and ask the students how the words in each column are alike. Introduce the term "short vowel" by saying something like, "These words have the short-a sound and these have the short-o sound." Children should note that each column has the same vowel spelling and sound except for the oddballs. Point out that these words all have a similar pattern called CVC that stands for consonant, vowel, consonant. The sort will look something like this:

Short *a*-cat	Short *o*-sock	Oddballs
sad	box	was
bag	mom	for
cab	job	
ran	got	
jam	fox	
ham	hop	
had	lot	
wag	mop	
bag	top	
map	hot	

5. Since these words can simply be sorted visually by looking at the letters in the word, the second sort should be done by **sound**. Keep the same headers, but this time the teacher should say the word without showing it. Students take turns identifying where the word will go and can check as soon as the word is placed in the column.

Extending: Students should get their own words for sorts and engage in the routines suggested earlier. We especially encourage you to have your students work with a peer partner or a parent in a no-peeking/blind sort.

Additional Words: *dad, lad, van, fan, sag, nag, lag, ram, yam, dam, lap, yap, map, jot, pot, mob, cob, cop, pop.*

SORT 39　SHORT *I* AND *U* IN EASY CVC WORDS

Introduce the sort following similar steps as in sort 38. Pictures for *i* and *u* are found in sort 35. Model the oddball category again with the word *put*. Talk about the name of the sounds (short-i and short-u) as well as the CVC pattern in all the words.

Short *i*-pig	Short *u*-cup	Oddballs
six	but	put
zip	run	
rip	cut	
bit	nut	
big	rub	
will	jug	
him	tub	
win	fun	
pin	gum	
did	hum	

Additional Words: *kit, lit, pit, fig, rig, bin, tin, bill, fill, pill, mill, hill, lid, rid, bud, hut, rut, hub, bum, pup.*

SORT 40   SHORT *E, I, O,* AND *U* IN EASY CVC WORDS

Introduce the sort following similar steps as in sort 38. Pictures are found in sort 36. The words *get* and *ten* may or may not be oddballs depending on local dialects.

bed	pig	sock	cup
yes	six	not	bus
let	hid	pop	mud
pet	mix	hot	cub
ten*	his		bug
wet	miss		sun
get*			
bell			

Additional Words: (see lists above for *A, I, O, U*) *bet, let, met, net, set, vet, bed, fed, red, well, fell, sell, yell, tell, beg, peg, leg, hen, pen, men, den, when.*

SORT 41   SHORT VOWELS *A, I, E,* AND INITIAL DIGRAPHS

Begin with an **open sort,** asking the students for their ideas about categories: "Who has an idea about how to sort these words? Is there another way?" These words should be sorted by the short-vowel sound but also by the beginning digraph; both of these should be modeled in the group. Reading these words will be challenging due to the initial digraph. Help students look at these words as onsets (in this case a digraph) and rimes they may have seen in previous sorts (*-at, -ip, -in,* etc.). They still fit the CVC pattern because a digraph is a consonant unit.

Note that *th* has two slightly different sounds in these words. In *than* and *that* the sound is voiced, and in *thin* and *thick* the sound is unvoiced. This difference is felt in the vocal cords rather than in the mouth and is often completely overlooked by speakers of English.

Short-vowel sort:

that	ship	when
chat	whip	check
than	chill	shed
shall	this	shell
shack	whiz	then
chap	chip	them
wham	chin	
	shin	
	chick	
	thin	
	thick	

Digraph sort:

ship	chip	whip	thin
shack	chat	wham	that
shall	chap	when	then
shed	check	which	them
shell	chill		thick
shin	chin		this
	chick		than

SORT 42   SHORT *A* AND *I* IN WORDS WITH INITIAL BLENDS

Introduce the sort following similar steps as in sort 41, sorting by the short vowel. In addition, ask students if they can see other ways to sort the words. In this case the words can be sorted by whether the blend has an *l* or an *r* and this will leave *skip* and *spin* as oddballs that do not have either. These words are complex due to the initial blend. Help students look at these words as onsets (in this case a blend) and rimes they have seen in previous sorts (-*ad, -ag, -in,* etc.) as well as more examples of the CVC pattern. The short-vowel sort will look something like this:

glad	drip
brag	flip
flag	slid
slap	clip
brat	drill
flat	grip
plan	slip
clap	grill
trap	skip
drag	spin
cram	
grab	
crab	
slam	

The sort by blends will look something like this:

crab	clip	skip
cram	clap	spin
brag	flap	
brat	flip	
grill	flat	
drip	flag	
trap	plan	
drill	slam	
drag	slap	
grab	slip	
grip	slid	

Additional Words: *clan, snap, stab, slab, swam, gram, skit, spit, skill, spill, trip.*

SORT 43   SHORT *E, O,* AND *U* IN WORDS WITH INITIAL BLENDS

Begin with an **open sort,** asking the students for their ideas about categories. These words should be sorted by the short-vowel sound but can also be sorted by the kind of blend as in sort 41. As in sort 41, these words may be challenging due to the initial blends. There may be disagreement with some short vowels due to dialect differences. Some children may choose to put *cross, gloss,* and *dog* in the oddballs. *From* is an oddball for most of us.

Word sort by short vowel will look something like this:

trot	sled	club	from*
plot	fret	glum	
drop	dress	gruff	
flop	bled	slug	
cross*		plug	
frog*		drug	
slob		drum	
gloss*		plum	
slot		`fluff	
		truck	

R blends and *l* blends:

cross	bled
dress	club
drop	flop
drum	fluff
fret	glum
frog	gloss
trot	plot
truck	plug
gruff	plum
	sled
	slug
	slob
	slot

Try combining all the words from the previous sort as well as this sort to review the five short vowels and the *r* and *l* blends.

Additional Words: *blob, clod, glob, plop, slot, crop, prop, spot, stop, sped, stem, step, spell, glum, plus, scum, smug, snug, spun, stub.*

SORT 44   SHORT VOWELS IN WORDS WITH FINAL BLENDS

Begin with an open sort, asking the students for their ideas about categories. These words should be sorted by the short-vowel sound but can also be sorted by the final letter or final blend. As shown, *lt, lk,* and *lf* are grouped together. *Half* is an oddball because only the /f/ sound is heard and it is not a true blend.

Sort by short vowels:

mask	desk	list	lost	just
ask	best	fist	soft	must
fast	nest	gift	cost	tusk
raft	left	milk		dust
past	melt	lift		
half	self			

Sort by final blend:

mask	fast	raft	melt	half
ask	past	left	self	
desk	best	lift	milk	
tusk	list	gift		
	fist	soft		
	lost			
	cost			
	just			
	must			
	dust			
	nest			

Additional Words: *disk, husk, risk, task, bust, cast, mast, mist, past, pest, rest, test, vest, west, blast, chest, twist, trust, sift, swift, shift, craft, drift, best, felt, tilt, wilt, shelf.*

SORT 45   SHORT VOWELS IN WORDS WITH FINAL DIGRAPHS

Begin with an open sort, asking the students for their ideas about categories. These words should be sorted by the short-vowel sound and the final two letters in the word. *Ss* is included here as a digraph. *Push* and *wash* are oddballs in this sort because they do not have the expected short vowel sound. Note: *Moth, cloth, toss,* and *boss* may not have the short sound depending on the regional pronunciation (/mawth/ or /clawth/)

Sort by short vowels:

cash	fresh	rich	moth	much	wash
class	guess	kiss	toss	such	push
grass		wish	cloth	rush	
bath		miss	boss	brush	
pass		with			
math					
path					

Sort by final digraph:

cash	rich	bath	class
fresh	much	math	grass
wish	such	path	pass
wash		moth	guess
rush		cloth	kiss
push		with	miss
brush			toss
			boss

Additional Words: *dash, dish, hush, mash, mesh, rash, sash, blush, clash, crash, crush, flash, slush, smash, swish, trash, mass, bass, pass, brass, glass, mess, bless, hiss, loss, cross, gloss.*

SORT 46   SHORT VOWELS BEFORE *NG* AND *MP*

Begin with an open sort, asking the students for their ideas about categories. These words can be sorted by the short-vowel sound but should also be sorted by the preconsonantal nasal at the end.

rang	jump
king	camp
sung	bump
sing	lamp
rung	limp
sang	stamp
ring	stump
bring	lump
wing	plump
swing	pump
hung	ramp
thing	
gang	

A building and blending lesson here might have students first make a word such as *cap* and then change it to *camp* to help them hear the very slight difference between those words. Words to contrast include: *rag/ran/rang, rug/run/rung, sag/sang, rig/ring, wig/win/wing, hug/hung, lap/lamp, pup/pump, rap/ram/ramp*

Additional Words: *bang, fang, hang, clang, slang, sling, cling, lung, tramp, damp, dump, champ, hump, rump, slump, thump.*

SORT 47   SHORT VOWELS BEFORE *NT, ND,* AND *NK*

Begin with an open sort, asking the students for their ideas about categories. These words can be sorted by the short-vowel sound but should also be sorted by the preconsonantal nasal at the end. *Want* is an oddball if you sort by vowels.

went	sand	junk
hunt	send	pink
pant	land	wink
want	wind	bunk
print	stand	bank
plant	blend	stink
spent		drink
		thank
		blank
		trunk
		think

A building and blending lesson here might have students first make a word such as *hut* and then change it to *hunt* to help them hear the difference between those words. Words to contrast include: *pat/pan/pant, sad/sand, lad/land, win/wink, bun/bunk, thin/think.*

Additional Words: *ant, chant, hand, band, grand, sank, spank, yank, drank, bent, dent, rent, tent, end, bend, mend, lend, spend, lint, link, sink, blink, bunt, runt, stunt, chunk.*

ASSESSMENT FOR SHORT VOWELS

A form is provided at the end of the short-vowel sorts for students to use. Call the following words aloud for students to spell. Evaluate each word for the short vowel as well as for the blends and digraphs that are included.

1. bell
2. box
3. gum
4. chin
5. shed
6. crab
7. clock
8. truck
9. nest
10. fish
11. flag
12. drum
13. plant
14. hand
15. ring

cat	sock	*oddball*
jam	sad	map
job	got	top
fox	hop	ham
had	ran	box
wag	lot	mop
was	for	hot
cab	mom	bag

Words Their Way: Word Sorts for Letter Name-Alphabetic Spellers ©2004 by Prentice Hall, Inc.

SORT 39   Short *I* and *U* Vowels

pig	cup	*oddball*
zip	bit	but
big	jug	pin
tub	rip	will
him	cut	rub
hum	win	fun
six	nut	run
put	did	gum

Words Their Way: Word Sorts for Letter Name-Alphabetic Spellers ©2004 by Prentice Hall, Inc.

bed	pig	sock
cup	let	six
hid	pop	not
pet	mix	his
mud	ten	yes
miss	cub	hot
wet	bus	bell
bug	get	sun

ship	chat	when
this	whip	shed
than	chip	chin
shin	that	them
wham	then	thin
chill	check	whiz
shell	shack	shall
chick	chap	thick

flag	slip	glad
clip	brag	flat
plan	drill	clap
grip	trap	grab
cram	drip	flip
crab	slid	drag
slam	slap	brat
grill	skip	spin

trot	club	sled
fret	plot	drop
glum	bled	flop
gruff	slug	plum
dress	cross	drum
plug	frog	drug
fluff	slob	truck
from	gloss	slot

ask	gift	best
fast	desk	lost
must	past	just
cost	lift	melt
raft	self	fist
milk	soft	mask
tusk	nest	list
left	dust	half

cash	rich	moth
class	path	boss
kiss	math	much
with	toss	wish
such	cloth	miss
rush	bath	pass
guess	fresh	grass
wash	brush	push

Words Their Way: Word Sorts for Letter Name-Alphabetic Spellers ©2004 by Prentice Hall, Inc.

rang	jump	king
camp	sung	bump
sing	rung	lamp
limp	sang	ring
pump	gang	ramp
bring	wing	swing
stamp	hung	stump
lump	thing	plump

SORT 47 Short Vowels

went	sand	pink
send	wink	hunt
bunk	land	bank
pant	junk	wind
print	stink	plant
blank	spent	blend
stand	drink	thank
trunk	want	think

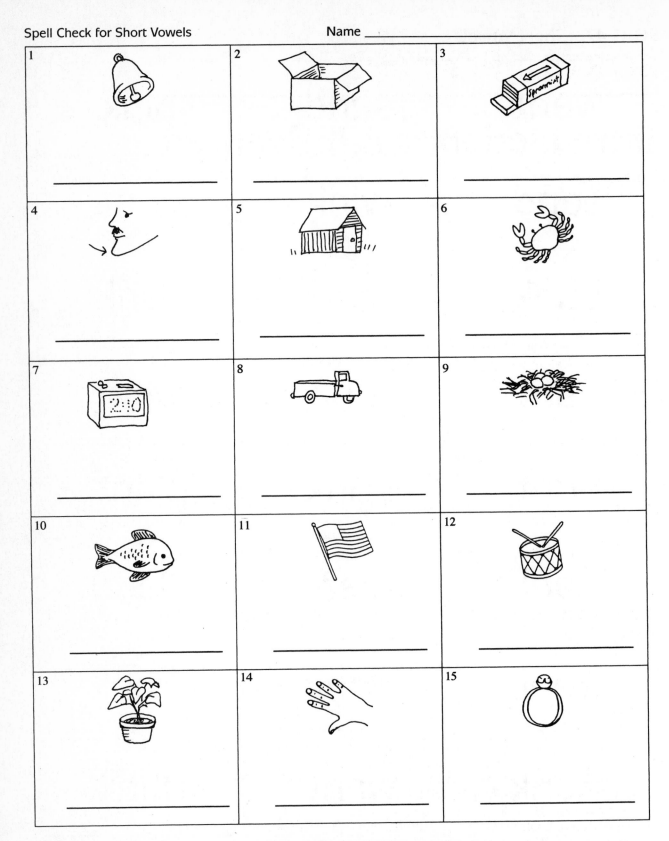

SORTS 48–49

Introduction to *R*-Influenced Vowels

NOTES FOR THE TEACHER

Single vowels that come before *r* are not short although they may occur in the CVC pattern as in *car* or *for*. Instead, these vowels have a unique sound and are referred to as *r*-**influenced** (or *r*-controlled). Since there are a good number of high frequency words that contain these sounds, it makes sense to introduce them after the short vowels in their simplest forms. They will be revisited during the within word pattern stage in more complexity. In these sorts, *or* and *ar* will be compared to short-vowel words as a way to draw students' attention to the *r* as a letter that influences the vowel that comes before it. **Note** that after *w*, the vowel sound varies as in *word, work,* and *worm* and in *warm, warn,* and *war*. Some of these words will be included in these sorts as oddballs but they are not really irregular because they correspond to a small but fairly consistent category.

These sorts can be used with students at the end of the letter name stage who have mastered short vowels as well as blends and digraphs. Typically these children are in late first grade.

Since this is a new feature and offers some new challenges, plan to spend about a week on each sort.

STANDARD WEEKLY ROUTINES FOR USE WITH SORTS 48 AND 49

1. **Repeated Work with the Words:** Students should work with the featured sorts several times including no-peeking/blind sorts and writing sorts described earlier and in *WTW*.
2. **Word Building, Blending, and Extending:** You may want to continue these activities described earlier if students have difficulty reading some of the words. However, in these words the *r* should always be chunked with the vowel. To build the word *short*, for example, you would segment it as *sh + or + t*.
3. **Reading:** Use decodable texts or little books that have a number of words with the featured vowel sounds. Be sure students can read these books with 90% accuracy on a second reading.
4. **Word Hunts:** Look for words in daily reading materials that mirror the featured vowel sounds. Word hunts can extend children's understanding when they include

longer words such as *party* or *story* that have *r*-influenced vowel sounds in one or more syllables.

5. **Games and Other Activities:** Look for games in Chapter 5 of *WTW* that can be adapted for *r*-influenced vowels.

6. **Homework Routines:** Parents can work with students in many of the same activities done in school. See Chapter 3 in *WTW* for a parent letter.

7. **Assessment:** A weekly spelling test may become part of your routine by the late letter name stage. You may also want to select words from the additional word list for testing to see how well students can transfer their mastery of features.

SORT 48   *OR* WORDS

Demonstrate, Sort, Check, and Reflect

Prepare a set of word cards to use for teacher-directed modeling.

1. Begin by asking the students to read over the words to see if there are any they do not know or understand. Ask what they notice about all the words. Probe until someone reports that they all have the letter *o*. Review with the students the sound they learned in words such as *sock* and *hop*—what sound did the *o* represent? Ask if all of these words have that sound.

2. Put out *sock* and *fork* as headers and read them, saying the words slowly to emphasize the sounds. Alert the students to watch out for two oddballs. Hold up a word such as *corn*. Ask the students whether it should go under *fork* or *sock*. Continue with student help until all words are sorted. *Word* and *work* are two high frequency oddballs. After saying each one slowly, help the children conclude that it does not go under either header because it does not have the right sounds and should be put in the oddball category.

3. After sorting all the words, read each column to verify that all the words have the same sound. Ask how the words in each column look alike. (They all have the CVC pattern but one column has only *or* and the sound is not short *a*.)

The final sort will look something like this:

fork	sock	Oddballs
for	fox	word
corn	drop	work
fort	rot	
born	shop	
sort	job	
torn	pond	
short	spot	
sport	trot	
storm	rock	
horn		

Additional *or* Words: *cord, cork, form, thorn, pork, torn, sword, snort, porch, north, horse, story, worm, worth, world.*

Challenge Words: (words that children can read and spell using familiar chunks) *morning, forgot, acorn, stormy, important, chorus, forest, forty, hornet, corncob.* You might ask children to read or spell these two- and three-syllable words as a special challenge and introduction to looking for familiar patterns in syllables.

SORT 49 AR WORDS

Introduce this sort in a manner similar to sort 48. Some of the short-*a* words have an *r* blend in them to challenge students to think about where the *r* comes—either before or after the vowel. *War* is an oddball in this sort.

The final sort will look something like this:

star	cat	Oddball
car	cap	war
farm	drag	
part	crab	
jar	snap	
bark	crash	
art	fast	
card	trap	
yard	rag	
shark	brag	

Additional *ar* Words: arm, bar, cart, far, barn, dart, hard, harm, tart, yarn, charm, chart, scarf, scar, sharp, smart, march, large, charge, dark, park, mark, spark, start.

Challenge Words: alarm, apart, cargo, carpet, harvest, market, party, starfish, yardstick, barnyard, charming, garden, darkness.

sock	fork	*oddball*
fox	for	corn
fort	word	drop
rot	born	sort
torn	shop	work
job	short	pond
spot	sport	storm
trot	rock	horn

Words Their Way: Word Sorts for Letter Name-Alphabetic Spellers ©2004 by Prentice Hall, Inc.

cat	star	*oddball*
car	cap	farm
drag	crab	jar
snap	bark	crash
art	war	card
trap	yard	rag
dark	brag	shark
park	fast	part

Sort 50

Contractions

NOTES FOR THE TEACHER

Contractions persist as a problem for spellers across a number of stages and you cannot expect mastery of them for some time. Some of the most frequent contractions are introduced in this sort in a simple manner and students can begin to understand how contractions are formed. We suggest teaching them at this point since students will be seeing them in their reading and using them in their writing. The words that make up these contractions have all been used in the sorts for late letter name–alphabetic spellers in this book. The placement of the apostrophe is not easy for young spellers to understand, but reading them seems to pose little trouble.

SORT 50   CONTRACTIONS

Demonstrate, Sort, Check, and Reflect

Prepare a set of word cards to use for teacher-directed modeling.

1. Begin by holding up a contraction such as *I'm*. Select the card that contains the matching two words from which it was made: *I am*. Model a sentence for the students using both *I'm* and *I am* (*I'm your teacher* and *I am your teacher*). Repeat this with another pair such as *can't* and *can not* (*I can't go home yet; I can not go home yet*). Ask the students if both sentences mean the same thing. Ask them why they think we have two ways to say the same thing. Someone may suggest that *I'm* and *can't* are a shorter way of saying *I am* and *can not*. Continue to match each pair and ask students to provide sentences that use both. Ask the students if they see any way that the word pairs can be sorted. A final sort might look like this when sorted by the words that make up the contracted form:

	I
I'm	I am
I'll	I will

	is
it's	it is
that's	that is
he's	he is

not

can't	can not
didn't	did not
don't	do not
wasn't	was not
isn't	is not

2. Students might be asked to cross out the letters that are dropped to form the contractions and introduced to the term **apostrophe.** They can see that one or two letters are dropped from the second word in each pair and replaced by the apostrophe.
3. Repeat the sort with the students' help, check, and talk about what they have learned about contractions.

Extending:

1. Students should get their own words to cut apart and sort for independent practice.
2. Word hunts will turn up other contractions (*what's, we're, haven't,* etc.) and students can be challenged to figure out what two words have been combined. Note that word hunts may also turn up possessive forms (*Pat's, Bill's*) so this may be a good time to briefly introduce that concept as well.
3. Writing sentences using both the contracted and noncontracted forms will help students understand the common meaning.
4. Concentation or Memory would be a good game to reinforce these pairs.
5. You can call these 10 contractions aloud for students to spell in order to check for mastery, but expect that they will continue to pose problems.

I am	can not
can't	that's
it's	I'm
didn't	don't
do not	was not
I'll	he is
that is	did not
wasn't	I will
it is	is not
he's	isn't

Appendix

Letter Cards for Building, Blending, and Extending
1. Word Families

b	c	d	f	g	h
j	k	l	m	n	p
r	s	t	v	w	y
z	sh	fl	fr		
at	an	ad	ap	ag	ot
op	og	et	eg	en	un
ut	ug	ip	ig	ill	

Words Their Way: Word Sorts for Letter Name-Alphabetic Spellers ©2004 by Prentice Hall, Inc.

Letter Cards for Building, Blending, and Extending
2. Digraphs and Blends

sh	h	s ch	c	th	
wh	t	st	sp	sk	sc
sm	sn	p	l	pl	sl
sw	bl	cr	fr	cl	fl
bl	br	gl	gr	pr	tr
dr	k	qu tw			

Words Their Way: Word Sorts for Letter Name-Alphabetic Spellers ©2004 by Prentice Hall, Inc.

Letter Cards for Building, Blending, and Extending
3. Word Families

at	ot	it	an	un
in	ad	ed	ab	ob
ag	eg	ig	og	ug
ill	ell	all	ick	ish
ack	uck	ash	ush	

Words Their Way: Word Sorts for Letter Name-Alphabetic Spellers ©2004 by Prentice Hall, Inc.

Letter Cards for Building, Blending, and Extending
4. Short Vowels and Final Clusters

a	e	i	o	u	
b	c	d	f	g	h
j	k	l	m	n	p
r	s	t	v	w	x
y	z	sk	st	ft	lt
lk	sh	ch	th	ng	nt
nd	nk	mp		or	ar

Words Their Way: Word Sorts for Letter Name-Alphabetic Spellers ©2004 by Prentice Hall, Inc.

Blank Template for Picture Sorts

Words Their Way: Word Sorts for Letter Name-Alphabetic Spellers ©2004 by Prentice Hall, Inc.

Blank Template for Word Sorts

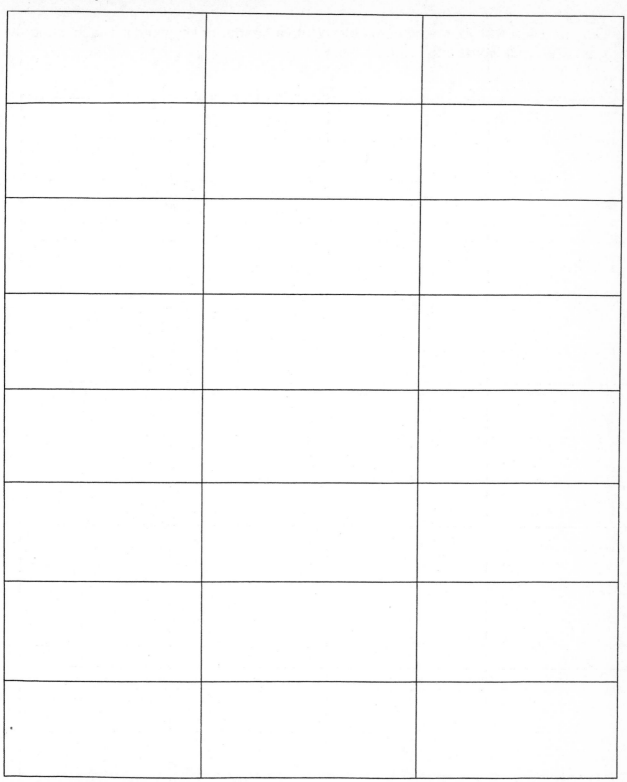

Independent Word Study Form

1. Cut apart and sort your word cards first. Write a header or key word for each category, then write your words into columns below:

_____

_____

_____

_____

_____

_____

_____

_____

_____

_____

_____

2. How are the words in each column alike? _____

_____

_____

_____

3. On the back of your paper write your headers or key words again. Mix up your words and ask someone to call them aloud as you write them under the correct header.